The Talking Horse
and the Sad Girl and the
Village Under the Sea

By the same author

The Curious Incident of the Dog in the Night-time

MARK HADDON

The Talking Horse
and the Sad Girl and the
Village Under the Sea

PICADOR

First published 2005 by Picador
an imprint of Pan Macmillan Ltd
Pan Macmillan, 20 New Wharf Road, London N1 9RR
Basingstoke and Oxford
Associated companies throughout the world
www.panmacmillan.com

ISBN 0 330 44002 0

A CIP catalogue record for this book is available from
the British Library.

Typeset by Macmillan Design Department
Printed and bound in Great Britain by
Mackays of Chatham plc, Chatham, Kent

To Alfie and Zack

*With thanks
to Don Paterson
and Sos Eltis*

Earlier versions of some of these poems appeared in *Acumen*, *Boomerang*, *Konfluence*, *Magma*, *Poetry & Audience*, *Poetry Review*, *Reactions*, *Stand* magazine and the *Evening Standard*. 'Poets' and 'The River-Car' were published in the Arvon International Poetry Competition Anthology 2000.

Contents

The Talking Horse
and the Sad Girl and the
Village Under the Sea

Go, Litel Bok

Ladies and Gentlemen, members of the jury.
Those of my trade, we are like the badger or the mole.
We work alone in darkness, guided by tiny
candles which we do not share, sweating to give birth
to replacement planets where things happen which don't.
And sometimes the hard jigsaw becomes a picture
and not a car accident. More rarely we place
our fingers adroitly on the frets or keyboard
and multitudes plummet through the small white trapdoor
which bears our hieroglyphs. Then we are taken up
into the blaze and shout of the conurbations
to make words in the air and strike the strange pose
from the clothing catalogue. But sometimes we see
a swallow in wintertime. And the talking horse
and the sad girl and the village under the sea
descend like stars into a land of long evenings
and radically different vegetables
and a flex is run from our hearts into the hearts
of those who do not know the meaning of the words
cardigan or *sleet*. And there is no finer pudding.
Now I am like that cow in the nursery rhyme.
The fire I have felt beneath your shirts. These cloisters.
Red mullet with honey. This surprisingly large
slab of Perspex. Your hands are on me. But this man
is another man. The clock chimes, my pumpkin waits
and the frog drums his gloved fingers on the dashboard.
May the god whose thoughts are like a tent of white light
above the laundry and the pigeons of this town
walk always by your side. My burrow calls. Good night.

A Rough Guide

Be polite at the reception desk.
Not all the knives are in the museum.
The waitresses know that a nice boy
is formed in the same way as a deckchair.
Pay for the beer and send flowers.
Introduce yourself as Richard.
Do not refer to what somebody did
at a particular time in the past.
Remember, every Friday we used to go
for a walk. I walked. You walked.
Everything in the past is irregular.
This steak is very good. Sit down.
There is no wine, but there is ice cream.
Eat slowly. I have many matches.

After a Beheading

When you have jumped the logging trains
across the Hendersons and eaten

stray dog roasted on a brazier,
when you think that you can feel

the rasp of a freshly laundered pillow
on your face and hear

the little song of halyards
below your window at 'The Limes'

but come round to the smell of petrol
and the sherry-hollowed faces

of your dubious companions,
when you want to lie down in the soiled,

grey snow and never move again,
you will come to a five-gabled house

in the suburbs of a cutlery-making city
and be embraced by a bearded man

with the build of a former athlete
who smokes 'El Corazon' cigars.

His wife will have perfect breasts
and make the noise of a leopard sleeping.

Neither of them will ask you for your name.
You will be offered the use of a bathroom

where the towel-glare hurts your eyes,
the soap is labelled in Italian

and the cream suit on the warmed rail
fits with sinister precision.

You will then be led into the dining room.
There will be beef Wellington and firm pears

and a jazz trio playing Monk
on guitar and vibes.

There will be many fingerbowls.
Your host will say, 'Eat . . . Drink . . .'

and as your hand hangs like a hawk
above the confusion of forks

you will realise that this
is where your journey starts.

Cabin Doors to Automatic

We take off in a lightning storm.
The big jets kick in and we climb
through blue explosions;
below the fuselage, moonlight
on the Solway Firth, the fields
of Cumbria, our *litel spot of erthe*
that with the see embracéd is.

This is how we leave the world,
with the heart weeping,
and the hope that distance
brings the solving wonder
of one last clear view
before that long sleep
above the weather's changes.

Green

Horace *Odes* 1:4

Spring and warm winds unlock the fist of winter.
Winches haul dry hulls down the beach.
The ploughman and his animals
no longer love the stable and the fire.
The frost no longer paints the fields white.

The moon is overhead. Cytherean Venus
dances with her girls. The Graces
and the spirits of the trees and rivers
stamp the earth while flaming Vulcan
tours the massive thunder-forges of the Cyclops.

It's time to decorate your oiled hair
with green myrtle or with flowers growing
from the soft earth. It's time to find a shady spot
and sacrifice a young goat to the woodland god.
Or kill a lamb if that is what he wants.

Death's sickly face appears at the doors
of shacks and palaces. Rich Sestius,
this short life makes a joke of long hopes.
Pluto's shadow hall, those ghosts
you read about in stories, and that final night

will soon be snapping at your heels.
And then you won't be throwing knuckle-bones
to win the job of drinking-master,
or ogling pretty Lycidas, who'll drive men wild
until he's big enough for girls.

This Poem is Certificate 18

When you open a collection of poetry or attend a reading you need to know that the poems you choose to read or hear are suitable for the audience.

To help you understand what a poem is like you can look at the certificate it has been given. This poem has been classified as 18. That means this poem is unsuitable for anyone younger than 18.

A poem with an 18 certificate may contain scenes of a violent nature. Carlos de Sessa burning at the stake, for example, his hot fat bubbling like porridge. Or Erymas, stabbed in the mouth, the blade smashing clean through to the brain so that teeth, bone and blood spray from his ruptured face. The slow death of a parent, often from cancer, is particularly common.

There may be sex, too. A man may be sucked off in a McDonald's en route to the airport, a babysitter may masturbate on the kiln-fired tiles of her employers' bathroom and an arsehole may be described in more detail than is necessary. The word 'cunt' may be used.

In a poem with an 18 certificate the syntax may be knottier and the meaning more opaque than in light, narrative or straightforward lyric verse. A phrase may have as many as four different interpretations, all intended for more or less simultaneous comprehension. Conversely, when the hedged sun draws into itself for self-quenching and these modalities stoop to re-enter the subterrane of faith, the intention may simply be to confuse the less intelligent reader. Sometimes a line or phrase is used simply because 'it sounded right'.

A poem with an 18 certificate may be written according to occult rules which are not made available to the reader. A parallel universe may be assumed wherein the expanded *inkling* undergoes an *allusion* and, at the climax of *frogging*, *binges* in the *Bermuda*. Some 18-certificate poems purport to be translations of work by Finnish and Romanian poets who do not, in fact, exist. In others a lightbulb may be granted sentience.

Like plumbers and dentists, poets are fallible, and the possibility of genuine nonsense cannot be ruled out. Unlike plumbing and dentistry, however, poetry is slow, frustrating and poorly rewarded work which fails more often than it succeeds and is therefore embarked upon largely by men and women labouring under a sense of almost religious vocation, grandiose self-delusion or some combination of both. As a result, many poems with an 18 certificate are written by people whose minds you may not wish to enter.

The language of a poem with an 18 certificate may be denser and more powerful than the language you are used to dealing with. And though it makes nothing happen it may, like a piece of ice on a hot stove, ride its own melting into your soul and bring you face to face with the madness of space.

It is an offence to read or supply a poem classified as 18 to anyone below that age.

Poetry certificates are there to help you make the right choice.

Trees

They stand in parks and graveyards and gardens.
Some of them are taller than department stores,
yet they do not draw attention to themselves.

You will be fitting a heated towel rail one day
and see, through the louvre window,
a shoal of olive-green fish changing direction
in the air that swims above the little gardens.

Or you will wake at your aunt's cottage,
your sleep broken by a coal train on the empty hill
as the oaks roar in the wind off the channel.

Your kindness to animals, your skill at the clarinet,
these are accidental things.
We lost this game a long way back.
Look at you. You're reading poetry.
Outside the spring air is thick
with the seeds of their children.

Nuns

They're out again,
flocking on the esplanade
like crows.

Passing the nudist beach
they giggle into cupped hands
like smokers round a match.

Some play crazy golf.
Some buy the less exciting
flavours of ice cream.

Others lie in deckchairs
and seem unnaturally comfortable
despite the heat.

Their ankles
are like flashes
of lightning.

We come across them
paired in bumper cars
or spellbound by cartoons

and Rugby League
on televisions stacked
in storefront windows.

They smell of soap
and dentists' hands
and rustle when they move.

Some go native,
as they always do,
stung by that long view

through the shilling telescope
or by the soft eyes
of the boy who rents the pedalos.

They move into cheap lodgings
with a single suitcase
and experiment with fashionable clothes.

Later, out of season,
we will recognise them,
frying breaded cod

or punching ferry tickets,
marked out
by the chapel-silence

which surrounds them still,
and by the way they stoop
to talk to children.

They are not mourned,
for come October,
when the ghost train shuts down

and the coloured bulbs along the pier
are packed away,
their places will be filled

by girls we teased in school
who yearned for love
and dreamed of reaching up

to take the teacher's hand
and being lifted from the flesh
in which they'd never felt at home,

or walking, as they walk now,
up the harsh rake of the lanes,
past burger bars and butchers,

past the Grand Hotel,
the Smuggler's Haven
and the Wall of China,

past the car park and the campsite,
past the Esso station
and the padlocked school

then through the granite arch
and over moonlit
geometric lawns

into the silence
of a clean white room
out of the swing of the sea.

Rescued

Horace *Odes* 1:5

Which under-muscled, over-perfumed boy
is groping you on roses in your love-nest,
Pyrrha? Who's inspired you to wash and cut
your honey-coloured hair like this?

God knows how many times he'll curse
the bad luck that made him love you,
and be flabbergasted by the force tens
blackening your little sea.

The idiot. He drinks your sunshine down
and thinks the wind will never change.
Those miserable men. You dazzle them
but no one ever ties up in your harbour.

As for me, you can read my story
on the temple wall: just another rescued
sailor who has offered up his sodden boots
to the great god of the sea.

1998

Come, Muse, let us sing of Velcro,
teabags and the Tetrapak.
For these too are works of nature,
as deserving of our praise

as dawn light on the Half-Dome,
hare tracks in overnight snow
or a fine French derailleur,
and will join the astrolabe

and toasting fork in old films
and stand on plastic trivets in museums,
giving off that low hum
of the long dead.

The Seventh Circle

Another werewolf night, the trees spastic
with wind and the dogs uneasy on their chains.
Three trolls wrestle with a bloody scrap
that will not die, the taverns roar and glitter
on the greasy quay and the Scissorman
chases the dragon down those little tracks
that promise daybreak by the sea, pistachio
cakes and minarets but curve, always,
back to that long night in the nursery.

The clock strikes twelve, and on the dirt road
where the shanties thin to marsh grass and burnt cars,
the music stops and tonight's crocodile
of lost children melt into the dark.
They are ours now. You cannot touch them.

They will see you in bad dreams.
The smoke of October bonfires, a single
gunshot hurling rooks into a white sky
and you, at the French windows, ogling
the gardener's boy while your niece makes a pig's ear
of a Chopin Polonaise and the servants
bitch about you in the scullery.

But you will see them from the evening train,
raging in burned-out lots and under bridges.
You will see them in the corridors
of hospitals. You will see them hover
on the dark that pools in hotel rooms
and lying under blankets on the tarmac
of the other carriageway, the broken glass
like snow and the lights flashing
like a black Christmas. You will see them
standing at your shoulder in the mirror.

They will not come back. The road is hard
and no one wants to listen to the stories
they will have to tell. But when the steel market
crashes and the orchard is paved over
and the bailiff's men are playing blackjack
on the stairs they will be waiting for you
at the bottom of the frozen lake.

A Tally Stick

The bark is notched six times, one notch
for every cow left in the pound,
then split, the cowman and the poundman
taking half each, so that when
the cowman comes to claim his stock
six cows are led out from the pound
though neither of the men can count.

Connemara, 1610:
A cowman spreads his hands and watches
as a priest names all his fingers.
He starts to count potatoes, hens,
the steps across his single field
whose blades the Lord alone can sum.

Then pausing at the gate one night
he thinks of seven. Not trees. Not dogs.
Just seven. Like The Plough
before God put the stars in.

The Model Village

Today an old man had a stroke
and crushed the signal box.
You can't ignore that kind of thing.

But on the whole
I try to see the visitors
as clouds or hills.

I am an old man
and I have learnt my lesson.
Only small things matter.

But the young are different.
They hear the talk of Birmingham
and Weston-super-Mare

and listen to the songs
of love and loss
on picnic radios

and dream of slipping
through the ticket office
after dark

in search of telephones
and discotheques
and Chinese restaurants,

a world where games of football
can be won
and lost,

where roads run to the ocean
and the ocean runs
forever.

They will understand in time.
Sit still for long enough
and everything will come to you.

We got a helicopter last year,
strung on fishing line
above the plastic lake.

This year we got our first
black residents.
(The Pattersons were overpainted.)

But the cows still graze,
the brass band still plays
Hearts of Oak,

the town clock
still reads
ten to two.

And when the night comes down
I sit beneath the awning
of the hardware store

and watch the universe contract
to thirty homes, a loop of railway
and fifty billion stars.

New Year's Day

I walk on powdered
shell for three miles
to the spur's blunt head
where, each year,
something of the ocean
slows and falls
and turns into a yard of land,
and something of the emptiness
we spin through
silts and settles
so that we can walk
a little further
out into the fog.

Average Fool

Horace *Odes 1:6*

The poet Varius can celebrate
your victories in high-flown verse.
Your bravery. The deeds done
by daring forces under your command.
By sea. On horseback.

I never write about that kind of thing, Agrippa;
grand themes like the black anger
of Achilles who refused to back down,
the homicidal family of Pelops
or the voyages of shifty Ulysses.

Poetic honour and my muse,
whose only weapon is the peaceful lyre,
won't let me blunt the praise
of either Caesar or yourself
with my ineptitude.

Who, in any case, could find the words
for Mars dressed in his steel tunic,
Meriones black with Trojan dust,
or Diomedes who teamed up with Athena
and became an equal of the gods?

Unscarred by love myself,
I write of banquets, and of wars
where girls stab young men
with their fingernails. Or if a little scarred,
then no more than the average fool.

Bushings

They lie discarded in the long grass
between the lighthouse and the kyle,
a yard of snipped-off wire
knotted round their necks.

At one end a white-washed room,
the fog of Woodbines, a terrier
and the fastness of the Norwegian Sea
running in a mildewed frame.

At the other, tanning salons,
the Winter of Discontent, banana fritters
and *Saturday Night Fever*.

Between them, humming in the cable,
buried under gales and static,
the lonely birthday greetings, requests
for Tunnock's teacakes and a claw hammer,
the bump and crackle of a coal fire,
the final maydays and the silence after.

Midas

You rarely hear the prologue –
where ants are marching from the window
to the crib, each one carrying
a grain of wheat to feed the infant king,

the meaning of the story still unwrapped,
the picture fresh as water in a clay jug
or a hot loaf not yet frozen solid
by the king's greed.

Thunderbirds are Go

The island of the billionaire philanthropist
was made of plastic and his wonderful machines
were only toys. True, there were moments

when the colours brightened as we cut away
to focus on a tea cup or a herd of antelope
in flight, and everything seemed real.

But they were shots from other films,
rapidly replaced by trees and skies
which looked like trees and skies but never quite rang true.

We had our brief adventures then relaxed
beside the pool, while in his mountain lair
our nemesis the foreign villain licked his wounds.

We filled the sky with vapour trails.
We braved the flaming rig and nursed the stricken jet
back home. We held our nerve and everyone was saved.

Now everything is real. This bungalow. The early train.
We mow the lawn and smoke a cigarette
and sit here waiting for the call that never comes.

Great White

Shark attacks were rare in Chapel Brampton.
I should have been afraid of paedophiles,
leukaemia or Neil Billingham
who lost his right eye when he lit
a can of underarm deodorant.

But when I lay awake at 2 a.m.
as headlights swept the Solar System
wallchart and the cooling pipework
shifted in the floorspace, something else
was moving through the dark beneath the bed.

Carcharadon carcharias. Six thousand
pounds of muscle powering a hoop
of butcher's knives. The only animal
that ate its weaker siblings in the womb.
Immune from cancer. Constantly awake.

And just as pious Catholics once fondled
strips of cloth soaked in the hot fat
of martyrs, I'd run my hand across
that photo of the fisherman from Cairns,
his belly opened like a can of plum tomatoes.

Even now, in lakes and rivers,
or ten yards off the beach at Swanage,
I remember what's inside us all
and sense, behind my back,
that grey torpedo entering the shallows.

Rings

Horace *Odes 1:9*

Look at soaring Mount Soracte
brilliant with driven snow,
the overburdened forest
and the streams in chains.

Thaliarchus, drive the cold away
by heaping kindling on the fire
then pour a generous double-handled
Sabine jar of vintage wine.

The gods will do the rest. They'll calm
the gales wrestling with one another
on the boiling ocean. Then the cypress
and the old ash will be still again.

Forget tomorrow. Cherish everything
chance gives to you today.
You're young, boy. Dance and love
while sour old age holds off.

Move quietly and hunt the squares
and courtyards at the hour of dusk
for squeals of laughter which betray
the young girls hiding

in the darkest corners.
Then slip the rings and bracelets
from their arms and fingers.
They'll complain. But not much.

Black

It comes as a surprise to find that hell
is the same house you've lived in these nine years.
Two orange stains beneath the kitchen taps,
birdsong in the yard, those floral curtains.
But you're not at home. Not by a long way.
That fist of wet meat in your chest
will not let you forget. The seconds pass,
as slow as that frozen age before the child
hits the red bonnet of the skidding car.
You light a Marlboro from the dog-end
of the last. Outside, shoppers and workmen
swim through their day like dolphins, ignorant
of how they do this stupid, priceless trick
you once knew. The phone rings. Your cigarette smoke
does its poisonous little ballet.

The Penguin

It's all too much. The white rhinoceros,
The common shoveller, the Cuban tree frog.
A whole world and every part of it
a short walk from the tea-room.

Pushchairs. Cornettos.
A basin of blue concrete
and a Humboldt penguin tumbling
in three feet of dirty water.

If only we could slip inside those eyes
and find our way back
to the pack-ice in the Weddell Sea.
Instead we move on to the gibbons.

The daylight hammers on and off.
Mountains explode,
bleeding black smoke downwind.
Tides pulse on the coast.

Tracks radiate
from settlements, leaping
the firebreaks of gorge and firth
to seed another, then another.

Forests burn.
Fields. Pipelines. Roads.
The brief nights
blaze like lava.

Lines blur. The lava cools.
Green takes it all back.
Forests thicken. Tides pulse.
The daylight hammers on and off.

Days

Horace *Odes 1:11*

Leuconoë, stop examining your
Babylonian horoscopes
and wondering what kind of death
the gods have got in mind for us.

We'll never know. Accept it.
This winter pummelling the ocean
on the pumice rocks of Tuscany
may be our last.

Or not. Be sensible and pour the wine.
This life's too short for longing
and the clock spins as we speak.
Days come and go. Hold on to this one.

The River-Car

The way it's parked, nose-down between the wet rocks
in the leaf-light of the gorge, water pouring
through the windscreen and the tyres blown;
as if the naiads put their fairy horses
out to grass and cruised the night in silver Escorts.

Or as if three boys from Hebden Bridge
grew bored and stole a car and drove it halfway
to the moors, grew bored again, then rolled it
from the muddy track and watched it hammer
through the trees until it came to rest

a hundred yards below. And as the echo
died away, the car they drove in dreams
kept floating downstream and the boys they'd never be
rode every bend of starlit water to the ocean.

Galatea

That first ripple in the marble.
Her hand on his wrist like a tame bird.
Her eyes opening. The big skylight,
the white-washed walls, the brace of chisels.

A baby's mind inside a woman's body,
playing *Peep-Bo* with a nurse, then bathed
and towelled dry and taken to his bedroom
as a sweetmeat when the guests have gone.

Christmas Night, 1930

The party's over. Downstairs the monsters
of cigar-smoke and society-talk
coil and uncoil among the tissue paper
and the tangerine peel.

This was your room once. The crib.
The mirror. Your painting of a flower.
Only the initials on the shaving kit
connect you to the man that you've become.

In the kitchen your mother's ghost
soaps the greasy plates and hauls
the turkey carcase to the pantry
so that she can scrub the table clean.

In the black square of the window
it hovers again. Dog or deer.
The animal that terrified you once.
But you can hear what it's saying now.

So take the curtains. Take the bowl
with blue stripes and the white cloth
on the dresser. Take the silence.
This is all you'll ever need.

Step across the sill and walk
into a night where the trees
are on fire and the stone church
dances on the dark.

Lullaby

for Edith (1908–2003)
and her great-grandson, Zack (2003–)

Starlight, star bright
Lie in this cradle of night
and sleep tight

Sea shell, sea swell
Ring the church bell
for all is well

Sundown, sunrise
Nothing dies
so close your eyes

The Twilight Zone

I'm in a tailback near Basingstoke,
pondering the sad-dog brakelights
of the V-reg Nissan up ahead,
thinking how we never got
the jet-packs or the protein pills
and how they'd be as unremarkable
as radios or Teflon. I'm thinking
of the way time runs just fast enough
to keep us entertained, but not so fast
we spend the whole day dumbstruck
by the fact that we can clone a sheep
or eat a mango in the Wirral.

Late October 1978.
We're smoking in The Friar's Grill
and playing with the cool, rotating cover
of my newly purchased Led Zep III
when, apropos of nothing, Nigel says
that Mr Rothermere's dead.
And sure enough, we find out later
that he died as we were talking,
falling down the stairwell of the school
we'd left five years before.

When we hear the news
we feel like hunters from the lowlands
of the Congo hearing Elvis Presley
on a Walkman, petrified
to think what devilry could squeeze
him into such a small box.

Which is when the sad-dog brakelights
of the Nissan just ahead go out,
the tailback dissolves, I put the Golf
in gear and boldly go to Basingstoke.

The Short Fuse

Horace *Odes 1:16*

More gorgeous daughter of a gorgeous mother,
burn my poems if they injured you,
or hurl them out into the Adriatic.
Nothing churns the human heart like anger:

not Apollo when inspiring the priestess
in the shrine at Delphi,
neither Cybele nor drunken Bacchus
nor his cymbal-banging followers.

And nothing, not the sword of Noricum,
not the ship-devouring sea, not wildfire,
not the terrifying storm of Jupiter himself
descending, holds it back.

They say Prometheus was forced
to use a part of every animal
when making Man, and put the short fuse
of the savage lion in our guts.

Anger bought Thyestes to his grisly end
and goads all conquerors to raze
great towns and arrogantly plough
their walls into the earth.

Don't let yourself be swept away. The same fire
burned in me when I was young, and wrecked
those golden days by driving me to write
those poems in the white heat of the moment.

But I would gladly change those bitter lines
into a sweet song and strike out every harsh word
if you would give me back your heart
and be my lover.

Miaow

Consider me.
I sit here like Tiberius,
inscrutable and grand.
I will let 'I dare not'
wait upon 'I would'
and bear the twangling
of your small guitar
because you are my owl
and foster me with milk.
Why wet my paw?
Just keep me in a bag
and no one knows the truth.
I am familiar with witches
and stand a better chance in hell than you
for I can dance on hot bricks,
leap your height
and land on all fours.
I am the servant of the Living God.
I worship in my way.
Look into these slit green stones
and follow your reflected lights
into the dark.

Michel, Duc de Montaigne, knew.
You don't play with me.
I play with you.

Woof

I'm in the manger, sleeping.
Let me lie.
You bite me, everybody wants to know.
I bite you, no one gives a damn.
Why bark yourself
and keep me in this hole?
You let me slip,
I fight, you call me off.
I'd speak in Latin
but I'd make a dinner of it.
So let me return, as ever, to my vomit.
All the guilty are in my house.
I'm sick, tired, gone,
the ugly girl, the ditched butt
of every cigarette,
every hard crust, every wasted evening.
Sit. Fetch. Heel.
I'm old. I cannot learn new tricks,
but I will have my day.
My star will rage
and I will match you step for step
in the midday sun
and haunt you in this black coat
through my watches of the night.

I'm your best friend,
but the more I get to know of you,
the more I like myself.

Gemini

You did the Hippy-Hippy Shake.
I messed with Mr In-Between.
Tonight you'll hit the first three chords
of 'Crazy' and a thousand tiny
lights will make you half-believe
the sky has fallen at your feet.
I'll watch a documentary
about the life of Cary Grant,
then take a bath and go to bed.

You'll blunt the come-down with some sweet
brown sugar in a five-star suite
and wake from the recurring dream
in which your third wife fucks the pool-boy,
and see, across the bed,
a tattoo stallion on the shoulder
of a girl your daughter's age
and hope she'll keep on faking sleep
until you're halfway to a strong
black coffee and a cigarette
in Mother Mary's Bar 'n' Grill.

I'll read the Sunday magazines
and find you bathing in that pop
and glare of being seen you've lived with
all your life, which burns and bleaches
everything until the route you took
and everyone you left behind
have turned to vapour trail and backdrop.

Did it have to be like this,
the future like a fault in flint
it took a hammer-blow to find?
Did you feel a different North
and peel away? Or was your gift
to slip the leash of every story
that we told ourselves to mend
the absence that you left behind?

This, for what it's worth, is mine:
I passed the bottle which said *Drink Me*,
but you drank, and grew and grew
until the town, your family
and friends were all too small for you.
And by the summer you were gone.

I wake some nights at 5 a.m.
and, shuffling to the window, see
a figure standing on the gravel
just outside the porchlight's range
and wonder what it is you want,
to mock me, or to make amends?
To come inside, or take my hand
and lead me to a black Mercedes
purring on the hill? To get
some measure of how many miles
you've put between us, or how few?

I feel the tug of gravity
which everyone who knows you feels,
but turn and potter back to bed
and melt into that larger dark
where you will always orbit, far out,
lord of hearts and oceans, lit
by sunlight borrowed from the far side
of the world, bright satellite
to this fixed earth, my counterweight,
my twin, my necessary ghost.

Old, New, Borrowed, Blue

The day we met.
This unexpected envelope.
My San Francisco Mime Troupe T-shirt which you wore
        to potter in the flat, whose sleeve-trim matched
Your eyes.

That sleepless night.
This sleepless night.
The face I'll wear to shake your hand and wish you well.
The way I'll feel when I do.

'Paper Moon'. Our song.
'Jesu, Joy of Man's Desiring'.
My *Ella Live at Montreux* which I hope he plays one night
                by accident and makes you cry.
This honky-tonk parade.

Dry Leaves

Horace *Odes* 1:25

Young men stumbling home from parties
don't throw pebbles at your windows now.
You sleep till dawn and that busy door
of yours now hugs the step. No one

asks how you can sleep when they are dying
all night long for love of you. Times change.
You're old and no one gives a damn.
You'll weep at all the men who have deserted you

as gales from Thrace roar down
that empty lane on moonless nights.
The hot lust which sends mares mad
will flare around your ulcerated heart

and you'll cry out at the young men
who love the ivy and the dark green myrtle
but who throw the dry leaves
into the East wind, that bride of winter.

Poets

They are seldom racing cyclists
and are largely innocent

of the workings of the petrol engine.
They are, however, comfortable in taxis.

They are abroad in the small hours
and will seek out the caustic blue liqueur

that you purchased in Majorca
for comedy reasons, and will rise late.

There are whole streets
where their work is not known.

Spectacles,
a father in the army

and the distance to the next farm
made them solitary.

Their pets
were given elaborate funerals.

No one understands them.
They are inordinately proud of this

for they have shunned
the brotherhood

of the post room
and the hair salon.

They write a word
and then another word.

It is usually wrong.
Their crossings out are legion.

They sit in trains
and pass through cotton towns at nightfall,

conscious of the shape of cranes
on the violet sky

and how the poured creamer
pleats and billows in their coffee,

and how both of these things
whisper, softly, 'Death.'

Silver Nitrate

The dead seem so authentic, posing beside
traction engines in their practical jackets
with their folk-songs and their knowledge of mushrooms.
But they were just like us, vain about the trim
of their moustaches and their Sunday shoes.
They, too, had the dream about the dark house.

Belonging is for horses. Home was always
in the past. The Labrador, baked puddings,
the long table in the orchard at Easter.

Meanwhile, we're stuck on this side
of the glass, watching dead leaves turn
slowly in the abandoned paddling pool,
remembering that winter when the snow
was so thick we built a cave
of blue light in the centre of the lawn.

The Facts

In truth, the dwarf worked in a betting shop
and wore an orthopaedic shoe.
The ugly sisters were neither sisters nor, indeed, women,
nor were they remotely interested in the prince.
The plain librarian looked better with her glasses on,
the bomb had not been fitted with a clock
and when the requisitioned farm-truck shot
the as-yet-uncompleted bridge it nose-dived
into the ravine and blew up
killing both the handsome sheriff
and his lovable but stupid sidekick, Bob.

The House of the Four Winds

A decimation of the novel by John Buchan

PROLOGUE

Philosophic historian,
chronicle that bleak night,
the corncrakes, the explosives,
the exact condition of the owl.
Deliver judgement on the breakdown
of the soul of the general manager
and linger over that summer
in the penitentiary. Alison,
I have not forgotten the ginger
cigarettes and Maurice's face
in repose. I was sick.
You civilised that solitude.
Fashion our private landscape
out of the world's howl.
Write me a cure in poetry.
Go far. Go too far.
Find that glimpse.

CHAPTER I – HEAT

The inn at Beechen.
Hot rye-cheese and onion bread,
a coarse red track
through beet-fields and water-cress.
No map, only moth and star

and pine, the German weather
pleasing but without glamour.
The peasants laughed. He could not.
Something was waiting for him,
a little havoc of exquisite blue eyes,
the kindness of puzzles
and the quarrels of politicians.
His heart spoke in an unknown tongue.

CHAPTER 2 – HUNT

Daylight and velveteen morning,
fried eggs and blue granite.
His mind was a dark stone.
Was there really a corpse?
Might not the purpose of the devil
be to break the plump and soft?
He rested for ten minutes
by the car factory
where Said was burned.
He had tasted the prince's hand
in Cairo. Bees, verbena,
agapanthus, that hot breath.
He had been filled. But after that?

CHAPTER 3 – FATE

Strawberries, turquoise snowdrifts,
satisfactory hot food, the same pumpkins

drying on the shingle, green water.
The afternoon enlivened by the thought
of being unpleasant in the sulphur baths
with her English friend. Letters
to Bolivia, Uruguay, Scotland.
The quiet cancelling-out of the soul.

CHAPTER 4 – DIFFICULT

Meaning is nothing. Nothing.
To understand you have to get down
into the meadow of twinkling lights.

CHAPTER 5 – GONE

The sun, the road, this earth,
the body, food, sleep, questions,
judgement, medicines,
a rifle bullet, endless walks,
the works of Walter Savage Landor,
public houses, veal, goat, tea,
good government, bad government,
old mischief, new brooms,
a woman shot against a wall,
a deal, an aeroplane, the logic
of events, that solemn river,
a tombstone over the border.

CHAPTER 6 – RAIN

They did not expect comfort.
They turned and stood
in the acetylene dazzle,
the gentleman queer
and the plain German dyke.
Her car was in disrepair.
He suggested coffee.
'I know you.' 'How?'
'The prince. That evening . . . '
Question. Answer. Bad news.
His blue eyes had a light in them
that scored the heart.

CHAPTER 7 – LESS

The delicacy of the situation.
The youth of a nation.
The toy shops of fame.
The old, fierce game.
Delirious applause.
Loyalty to the cause.
The smoke of a train.
The cornfield plain.
The wolf's cup.
Farm boys strung up.
The heart a stone.
The years alone.

A photograph of a face.
The mercy of the human embrace.

CHAPTER 8 – MEND

The sack over his head.
His last minutes,
treated as a common dog.
A toilet, blood,
two smoking wires.
A memory of Cambridge,
soda water on the terrace,
a sleepy cat.
The sound of triggers
at the back of his head.
An open window.
Guns. A turtle-dove.

CHAPTER 9 – NIGHT

We expect a pattern,
but the only song
is a crazy noise
of philosophy and accident,
calamity and transformation,
a rare black comedy
of hideous things
and ragged lights
in an adjacent field.

CHAPTER 10 – AURA

So small a thing
that little room of sleep,
yet it was sealed to him.
He walked the empty street.
Hot breath of baking.
Garbage in the gutters.
A bicycle. The derelict
torches of the stars.

CHAPTER 11 – BLOOD

Sea-sick, light-headed,
the swell strong, the honeycomb
clouds scattering. Time
telescoped. Mere antique dust
her lovers now. She was a wolf,
exotic, reckless. Women
were like horses, to be broken.
The troubled girl with amber hair
that she had forced, the trembling
countess, Janet, picturesque
Miss Squire . . . That desperate
hot trust. Her heart poised
like a falcon for the swoop.
The wild relief of sex.

CHAPTER 12 – ROPE

The English had the house under observation
and had come to certain conclusions.
It was done circumspectly so as not to alarm.
There was no evidence of human presence.
But what was the meaning of the distant bells?
That horrid certainty. The halted, faint notes.
Spilt lime. A spiral staircase. Light.
A door unlocked. Inside, rotting boards
and paper dropping from the walls, the odour
of a barber's shop, the slow turn
of the monstrous gargoyle and that click,
as if a clock were running down.

CHAPTER 13 – HOME

The city sparkled in the sunlight
as a waiter brought the morning paper.
From it stared a face of . . . Oh,
it was ridiculous. Her nerves,
the doctor said, were frail.
He was civil, God be praised,
if whisky-scented. But . . . that man
was so familiar. His name was . . .
what? Beard, morning suit . . .
She hesitated. Something stirred
on the horizon, scarlet, blind,
immense. A distant groundswell.
One long blaze of men and women

kissed and rapturous, that roar
of thousands in the heart.

ENVOI

Almost dark. The last moraine.
Uplands, twilight, prospect.
Lights, cars, baggage.
You have had your dream
and felt the spell of ordinary
things made young again.
You can be mortal now.

Once Upon a Time

Some want to know what happens
when the bent cop holds a switchblade
to the pimp's throat. Some want
to see a horse the colour of conkers
or hear the boom of fireworks
like carpets being beaten.
Others want to stand, invisible,
beside a bed as two men fuck,
or cheer when the little deaf girl
kicks the fat priest who is every
bully they have ever known.

But everybody wants to slip
their flesh off like a winter coat
and enter this familiar room
that smells of gas and beeswax,
where sunlight pours from the big window
and the freighters move continually
in the river's mouth.